all of her pain

Alexandra Heather Foss

DEDICATION

For my parents, who gave me life,
and who give my life love and meaning.

Everything I have is thanks to you.

ACKNOWLEDGMENTS

Many people, places, and things, define who we are, how we feel, and what we love. Each person we encounter offers us something, some form of learning, or experience, that helps us to evolve. In that way, even when someone hurts us, they also have helped us, to be stronger, or more resilient, as we develop our personal power.

Everyone in my life thus far deserves at least some gratitude, because I wouldn't be who I am without all associations, but some are of course more significant. These are the people who love, and stay, even when I am not that lovable or likeable. The people who have dramatically impacted my emotional, spiritual, physical, and sociological growth, for either my entire life, or for a large portion of it.

I will elaborate on this list with each volume of poetry and writing I publish, but for this first book, I want to thank the core group of people, actively a part of my life. Only a few continue to show up with their love, regardless of season, or circumstance, letting me know with their presence, that I am loved, and valued.

Since conception, my mother, Pamela, has been the one person I can always count on. I know what love truly is because of the example she sets. She is warm, and nurturing, intelligent and fun. She is full of so much life it is like the whole universe exists within her, all that energy and emotion, and her artistic and musical heart are the colors and beats of my life. She is more than a mother, and now Nana to my son, she is also my dearest friend. If I didn't have her, I wouldn't be me. Not on any level. I have her to thank for infinite blessings.

I also am grateful for my father, Warren, Grandad to my son. He has allowed me to be, and heal, and write, at my own pace, and in my own way, while never pushing me to be anything other than myself. He is a generous man, who has provided for his family a beautiful life, by working hard every day of his. I love him, and that I am half of him.

My son Oliver is my wish come true. Should no others be granted, he is the one thing I most wanted from this life. A child. My child. My lovely little boy. He has shown me what it means to selflessly love, and be devoted entirely to someone. And in my life, I have never laughed more, than when I am with him. Being his mother is my favorite thing, over every other personal passion, and every time I look into his rainbow eyes, I see the eternal why. Why I am here. Why we all are.

My grandparents are a cherished part of my story, who I always miss. Grandpa, Nanny, Grammy, Grampy, and Dottye. Five people this world is lacking without. They were fun, interesting, loving, dynamic people, who loved family, gardening, learning, nature, cooking, and laughing. They expanded my heart, with a love that will always be there, and they are some of my favorite parts of life.

For every single person who has been a part of allofherworld, since it began in July of 2018, thank you for your care and time. You have been here for me, when I needed you most, and I appreciate you all. We may not know each other in person, but you are the reason this book exists. Without an audience of supportive people, a writer does not evolve into an author. So thank you for making me one. You have helped me realize a lifelong dream.

PREFACE

I was born an artist. I knew it, digging my toes into the sand, during hot Cape Cod summers with my grandparents, and when I told my Maine grandmother at five, I was going to write for a living. Sometimes we are called in a direction, and that is simply it for us. Art, for me, is living, it is loving, it is wind through the leaves to the side of my house, and sucking the sweet flesh from a ripe slice of mango, where the air smells like tiare flowers. But the journey has been a process, like I suppose everything is. And the journey of this book started for me at the end of December, in 2016.

That year nearly ended me. I experienced a heartbreak so crushing, so complete, that I couldn't salvage hope. Everything felt gone. Past, present, future. I was in my mid-thirties and it took losing my partner of half a life to realize things like how absolutely I wanted children. I kept thinking, before that, I had the luxury of time. That there was no rush, no urgency. But then the choice felt gone, and I realized nothing, no honor, award, or accomplishment, none of it would mean anything to me at the end of my life, could I not be a mother.

I was lucky that October. I met one of only two men I have romantically loved. He was this handsome breath of fresh air, that was unlike anyone I had ever known, and when I was with him, for the first time in my life, I was completely present. I felt alive and excited and sure. Sure that this was what every previous step in my life had been leading me to. To him. To whatever we would create together. Which ended up being my son.

Right before the new year, not even a week before my son was conceived, I composed a letter to the Universe, a plea and a prayer, really. I asked for my child. I didn't know who or what I was writing to, if anyone or anything could hear me, but I wrote out all the words that filled that wish.

I believe in destiny because I met his father, and because my son Oliver heard me. He has told me that often, in our house, how he came to me, falling from the angels into Mommy, and even if he couldn't speak, or doesn't accurately remember, I know that is what happened. And I am so lucky that he did. His life from conception to now has been my most creative and fertile period. Everything in this book, it all has been since him. I may have been born an artist, but life has also made me one, with every trial and triumph.

That following year, during my pregnancy, I started writing poetry. I had been an essayist throughout college, more into analytical papers, but this was purely creative. I didn't even know the correct form, only that I had to get these words out, and in a way that they could fit into tiny squares and rectangles on Instagram. I had joined October 10th of 2016, the day I met his father, and I began to learn this whole community of artists, poets, and writers, who share of their souls every day with others.

This was my tribe. I could feel it. So I started to share, through allofherworld. It was a secret then, something I didn't tell anybody I knew about. I just wanted to connect, with others like me, anyone who might be able to understand my heartbreak and longing. What it is like to love together, and alone, when there is safety, but also absence. Most days since then, I have shared some piece of my soul, or heart. There are words that come together better than others, but all of them are a part of this journey, of rainbows and storms, light and shadow, of what it means to be imperfectly human, while connected to others.

And slowly, though not everything has happened as I might wish, in terms of my personal life, I am piecing together a kind of healing. And because of every one of you, not only the people I know who love me most, I am a stronger, wholler, more creative woman. A portrait of human art, in dynamic motion.

I have chosen to keep these poems and other writings as they were originally written, with only small occasional alterations. That way, the integrity of the work remains intact. I have, however, included some extra pieces of creative writing, either from my Instagram stories, or my life outside allofherworld, as bonuses for those of you who have chosen to make this book a part of your library.

As far as the order, that comes as it felt right while assembling the book. I hope it flows in a way that speaks to you, and that you enjoy all of these lovingly prepared pages. As I have, writing them.

Start with honest.

The body of the pangolin is covered in keratin scales, that when illuminated make the shy, modest creature look as if it is draped in fabric iridescent like the inside of an oyster shell. Snow leopards are majestic felines with warm beryl eyes, able to withstand frigid temperatures and poached habitats. Cairn terriers have silky coats, sweet faces, and sharp minds, their tiny bodies sturdy as their wills. And fireflies burst into night with sunny determination.

It is easy for me to see the natural world as beautiful. The feathery arms of the weeping willow sway with the wind, spirited yellow buttercups bud in summer amidst otherwise green stalks of grass, the rose in any color is so intricately layered and textured that even when petals fade and fall the flower remains elegant. Every strawberry and every cloud have a beauty unaffected and unafraid, even when they are plucked and poked, and never does the okapi try to be the zebra, the wild horse the ladybug on her nose.

However complex the kingdoms of flora or fauna, there is a consistency and constancy to each living being. A seed slowly sprouts into a tree and birds use its branches to sing ancient melodies, but never does a datil pepper seed spend its life trying to blossom into a tomato. There is a certain acceptance inherent that humans seem subtracted from, and on some level life seems easier. Perhaps more biologically dangerous, but less socially so.

Insecurity is a prolific breeder in our species. Humans are hungry for love, and after a certain age, love becomes harder to find. Disappointment and disenchantment want us to believe less in ourselves and more in them. We become less cellular and more reflected, either by mirrors made of glass, or by human eyes. The process of consciousness that individuates us also threatens us, because we are not contained the way we are in the womb, and therefore are at greater risk. And the faces we are born with, of innocent purity, can easily become lost.

We are liked, or we aren't.

We are chosen, or we aren't.

We resemble the figures in our popular culture, or we don't.

We are unable to cocoon ourselves with keratin scales and everywhere, especially in this age of social media, someone has something we don't – security, safety, home, place, contentment, success, satisfaction. The process of comparison strips us of our identity, and then our power, and because we have become such shredded versions of our natural selves, it is difficult to know, even when we find someone or something that kind of resembles home, whether the attraction is superficial or authentic. Who we are is indeterminate.

My quest for reciprocity has been expensive. I have starved myself, scarred myself, trying to sculpt of myself someone that will be loved. But whether I am more myself, or less myself, seems not to matter. It will forever remain true that you cannot make someone love you who doesn't, nor can you carve from the ether the person who could. Whether I am true to myself or fake or kind or vicious, external love, in particular romantic, is not guaranteed. Nor will the skin I am in ever reflect fully all my varied and opposite truths. Some see a beauty queen, others a misfit, some see healthy, others see sick. I tell people I am on the spectrum and either they say "Of course," or "No, you aren't." Whether my lips rise or fall, inside there nearly always is a tear holding hands with drops of joy. People see who they want to see, more often who they need me to be, so they feel better about themselves. And the process of trying to prove myself, as if I am on trial, is exhausting.

I envy the wind. I envy the willows. I envy how they are asked to the dance.

My whole body felt like the inside of a lava lamp, shifting with fluid energy, as two made one, and one became two. My entire pregnancy I felt this incredible connection with a baby whose body and face were only a two-dimensional black and white image on a sonogram. To be that at peace, that connected, and undivided, even though by definition, I was, with someone else growing inside me, that is what I hope every day for.

Contentment with what is, and what will never be.

Discarded

may you never know
what it feels like
to be discarded
to become
the forgotten memory
of a heart.

Hidden Hollows

So much can be hidden.
Our emotional landscapes,
the dreams we
go to on our own,
the hurts we suffer,
and inflict on others,
what we yearn for.
Perhaps if ever the day
could safely come,
when secrets
lost their lustre,
more of who
we intimately are
could be seen.
And wouldn't
that be comforting?
To be accepted wholly,
without revision,
or condition.
In my hidden hollows,
that is the dream.
I see you.
You see me.
And we aren't going anywhere.

Primal Hunger

I know better.
And yet,
I hunger for you
like soil hungers for seed
in a field of forgotten flowers
we are but two
blossoming together
no resistance.
Desire pools like rain
into my roots,
sweet nectar
skating along my stem
you leaf around my curves,
you catch my petals
when they fall
I want you.

I want you.
When they fall
you catch my petals
you leaf around my curves,
skating along my stem
sweet nectar
into my roots,
desire pools like rain
no resistance.
Blossoming together
we are but two
in a field of forgotten flowers
like soil hungers for seed
I hunger for you
and yet,
I know better.

A Tremulous Thing

It is a tremulous
thing, the start
of a new day.

The destiny of a
moment unknown,
until it has passed.

I pass, from room
to room,
in this empty house,
as if somewhere,
in the shallow
corners, a small
beetle, perhaps
the bird in the
tree outside, can
offer me

some unbidden truth,
that will make
all the questions
I have,
without answers,
obsolete.

Forever

Forever
never
meant
for now
for me.

Controlled Burn

Heartbreak
hollowed me out
like an empty grave
but I refused
to be buried.

Light as the phoenix
from the ashes I
lifted into the light
of the October moon
in a glade where
fire lit by new love
hot as starlight
controlled its burn

wildly spreading
inside me seeds
into the spaces
where you,
had left me,
barren.

Casual Culture

our casual culture
cuts connections
coldly
compromising
our capacity
for compassionate
and constant
care

Do Lips Forget

I wonder
do lips forget
how to kiss
after so long
being alone
or is the way
written in
their lines
like a map
leading home

Beating

some hearts
never heal
they just
keep beating

So Easy

The soft as red velvet
decibel of your voice,

the water glass you
brought me every night,

how we laughed
wine tasting in Sonoma,

how words could fall
for hours from our lips,

it was easy for me
to love you,

and so easy for you
to leave.

Urgent Longing

The wind
waits
with urgent
longing
for someone
to see it
and not run
from
its husky
roar.

Requited

I wonder
what love
requited
feels like.

Burning Bridges

Some use wood
others use stone
but my future
walls are built
with the bones
of burning bridges.

Stranger

I knew your face
better than I knew my own,

but on that
fatal final walk,

down a bent road
bleached of color,

when you looked at me
you were a stranger.

Someone I Can Run Wild With

embers of desire
sometimes burn me
indelicate longing
the animal
I leave untamed
inside my skin
are claw marks
she hates to be caged

I wait

howling for a moon
that does not come

and someone
I can run wild with

Shadow of Who

The shadow of who we once were
I glimpsed at that station
one outlined figure
made by hands and lips
meant to touch
I carried my baggage
down the foggy lane of memory
until I realized it was you
half of that embrace
and she the woman
you left me for.

Love and Sex

If my heart could move on
my body would follow,
but for me love and sex
have always meant the same thing.

I Hate That

Thoughts of you
open and close my days –
I hate that

I defend you faithfully
knowing I deserve better –
I hate that

What we had rules over
what I could have –
I hate that

You are the ghost
but I have the unfinished business –
I hate that

I love you too much
to hate even your worst –
I hate that most of all

Lusty Love

was it love
or just
a lusty
hunger
for survival

Out of Touch

The minutes are devoured by days.
I lie in a knot of sheets,
time wrinkling the past,
memory a cold companion
to share a bed with.

I want to be held,
to feel the sure caress
that once you offered me,
but out of touch,
I have only my own hand
to reach for
in the darkness.

A Pen Unpressed

There was love
once, I am sure,
but now there is
only pent up
lonely longing,
like ink in a
pen unpressed,
leaning for paper.

Mercurial

I was too blinded by love
to see you as mercurial,
the inky drip
that has no fixed form.

I wanted solid
but still I reached,
even though never could I
hold you longer
than your fears,
and only could you ever
reflect my core temperature.

As All Things Wild

my shell had no cracks
shadows encroaching a space
never quite my own
I waited with a stalwart heart
full of undomesticated dreams
for a pregnant wind
coated with dandelion wishes
the release that came finally
felt like plains opened by horses
remember me like that
not trapped inside my skin
remember me as all things wild

The Heart Remembers

be strong but remember
so fragile we are
like paper we rip
with shredding words
stained like ink
the hurts that dig in
pain a metal pen
scratching into soul
a deeper tear
on skin wounds open
and scars close them
but not here
here the heart
remembers how it feels
being ripped apart

What Is Real

I often wonder what is real
is it the butterfly wing
the wrinkled face
how a nest slowly builds
the words you sold me
can the leg of a steed
form a more solid truth
than all my firing synapses
do I even have the courage
to receive the answer
when we are gone
from the skin of this lush place
will tears water its soil
can I know my impact
will I sink into forever

Not in Charge

tomorrow could be
an adventure
a step into
a new future
where my past
is not in charge
but I am scared
of what I will find
and of all
I will leave behind

For a Moment

a lilac snow
frosted the leaves
when last I saw you
in your arms boxes
in my womb life
the seasons stack
from then to now
and there you were
today beside me
crickets croon
into a halcyon sky
a love song meant
for the moon
and I think
how nice it was
to for a moment
not be homesick

My Heart of You

newly cut grass
a fleck of lemon
the scent of rain
puddling the earth
you were fresh
air needed to breathe
but a moment
in a time long ago
the glass gathers sand
a small mountain
I hear the seconds pass
unprepared am I
for how to rid
my heart of you

From where I sit I see a screen.
Though not the window I would choose,
it is a beacon, guiding me through
this curling storm of indigent thoughts,
that roll like waves much taller than I.
How dark these nights alone have become.
Even the moon is in shadow.
I step outside but nothing is familiar,
I a stranger in my life.
Is this home
or just a house to rest my head in?
Am I real?
Inside the cavity of this room
I cannot tell.

Understood

Into matter I shape time
stripping secrets
suffocating my soul
from this selkie skin
I scribble into these pages
with gentle force
stories softer on my senses
salvaging sacred treasures
from a scratchy past
I dream in the cradle of night
of a life not lost to translation
of a love that shelters
and is not rife with dread
to not with threat of withdrawal
be asked to be different
but to at last be understood.

Submission of Hubris

I chose us and into the sunset of old age
would always have I been yours
you saw our shapes more like shadows
not hewn of mortar or bone
and flesh was what divided us
perhaps I was standing still
a statue of unspent desires
unaware I could not move
I felt with you at home
my fears left like shoes at the door
and with you went the air
I needed to breathe
how I now am still standing
shows less an act of courage
but rather an exhausted submission of hubris

Pain As Art

what is poetry
but pain as art

Haunted by Chimeras

on parallel planes
exist two ghosts
that of my heart
stake territory
I bleed love
trying to fill
their skeletons
with substance
but I am tired
of being haunted
by chimeras

Heavy

you are heavy
like water
in my lungs
I cannot breathe

like water
in my lungs
I cannot breathe
you are heavy

in my lungs
I cannot breathe
you are heavy
like water

I cannot breathe
you are heavy
like water
in my lungs

Antique

I feel sometimes
like an antique
in the dusty corner
of a cluttered shop

To Your Lips

one day the wind
will carry my name to your lips
I hope not with regret

Macadam

tit for tat and my heart
like yours is macadam
a thick floor of broken bits
beneath a thousand footsteps
blocking one world from another

Exorcism

I exorcise you
with every line

How Colorful Loss Can Be

the wind sweeps up rivers
of gently falling leaves
the sound rustling me
from your dreamy kiss
cold I lie in bedsheets when
for years I lived in summer
of roses and hibiscus
and lush less lusty blooms
here summer empties
into winter's snowy mouth
how colorful loss can be

Unrequited

I love you
You love her
She loves him
He loves me

Wars

wars we fight
with ourselves
and others
to be free
and how lucky
when we are

South of Surrender

I fell south of surrender
and grew strong in love
but I am not as tall as the trees
who battle the seasons standing
their bark has no bite
leaves buttercup and bittersweet
collect like winter moonlight
in soft piles
my battles are septic
bodies scattering
like discarded summer blossoms
filled with poison

Reflected Light

I love you like this
with these words
in these memories
but you are reflected light
from my heart
should you return
I may not recognize you
to call you mine

None of This Is True

there is nothing I had to survive
monsters dressed in regular clothes
never threatened my safety
no nightmares invade
there is no one I am scared of
I am confident and content
I do not get left behind
I miss no one
I feel loved

One Day

one day the pain of after
will outweigh the good of before

Love Should Give

love should give
not take away

Before I Could

you cracked open my shell
and for you I wanted to pour out
but you were gone before I could

A Place to Land

so often in my life
I have felt
like I am circling
from above
searching for a
place to land

Then and Now

if only then and now
were not so far apart

Just Like That

I was unpopular
but in plump berries
and the flush glow of Christmas
how it felt to be read to
by a mother who really wanted me
and held by a Debussy song
I felt loved by life

and just
like that,
everything had
changed.

one hand touched me
then another and another
I could not breathe
choking on the memory of before
learning sex as pain
devoid of love
I lost my innocence
gaining in between a numbing fear

people joked I should kill myself
that they would if I refused
but I held on
wishing for the day
when I could leave them all behind
for a land with sunshine
and no shadows

Rise

you left me
crumpled
on the floor.
from there
I only could
rise

A Rare Thing

loyalty is a rare thing
in this casual culture

you are angry
and skittish
like a lion
that has gone days
without a meal
when have you felt home
have you ever
curled inside arms
that want only
to hold you
are you tired
of running
of defending
your position
on ice thinner
than the space
between lovers
could you ever
will you ever
believe in
answered prayers
I loved you
that was real
but what is love
on a one-way street
a couple walls
eggs on the stove
a child waiting
a bed half warm
me waiting for you
waiting for something
like a yesterday
that becomes
a tomorrow

Our Last Hug

had I known
that would be
our last hug
I would have
held you longer

ours is a world canopied by stars
below cerulean infuses the seas
amber ages the tears of trees
pink paints cheeks with passion
lemongrass seasons meals between strangers
bittersweet is the heart that breaks
caramel coats an apple shared by lovers
into winter ivory chalks her canvas
iridescent is the dewy afterglow of dawn
that sunshine rich does sparkle
we are a planet bursting with color
black, white, yellow, brown, green
they are our primary, primal language
the face that fills a space full of holes
into them we may lean and must when
our lives have been swallowed by shadows

Split Between

are we fractured
is it our destiny
to be in pieces
to not be whole
split between
continents of time
thought and space
why does what
others think
get to rule
over what we feel

A Simple Wish

it is a simple wish
someone I can be
fully myself with
who can do the same

Edited

I do not want to be edited
by a world with an eager red pen

Tiny Tales

these tiny tales
are me telling stories
of how I did not end

Where Is Love

where does love go
when it leaves a heart

The Good That Was You

so much has felt bad
maybe that is why
the good that was you
still stands out

Fear

I have never known fear
like when I thought
you were dead inside me

He Found Me

I was lost
when you left
and he found me.

Where Do the Marigolds Go

you are older now
stories etch your skin
like trees with many rings
where do the marigolds go
when fall has faded
how cruel this earthly cycle
that clears forests for new growth
and of babes makes orphans
when into the mist of memory
you gather moments
how will I go on
love starts with your name
since that newborn cry
you are my guide and shelter
I never want to miss you

hope that you exist
waters my lands
so dry I have become
in your absence
I want to be held
inside the dawn light
to have one plus one
equal a living infinity
how does it feel to kiss
to sing heart songs
with the skin
the years abandon
me these memories

Something Shifts

the new year nears
and something shifts
from letting go
to moving forward
you traded our forever
for a bag of beads
and in that deal
sold me the belief
that it was me
unworthy of you
but how could that be true
when lies are your truth
and my love is honest

you lost your home
you wander ravaged
a desolate landscape
for the familiar
do you wonder
if you are alone
does your daily search
starve you of more
than an empty belly
when was the last time
you felt full
the ice has melted
but that will
never warm you
only can the hope
that if you walk
far enough forward
your feet may reach you
where you need to be

My Love is Color

no one will
ever love you
as much as I do
for who you fully are
but my love is color
and you are in
black and white

for so long
I have felt ordinary
a mass of unmet dreams
and potential unrealized
fighting to be seen
praying to be chosen
fearing that my time
may never come
it is my sincere hope
that before I die
I know how it feels
to be content
with however I am
and whatever will be

If Our Love Were True

how do I tell my heart
what my head already knows
that if our love were true
I would not be here waiting

I imagine you there,
putting down roots,
in some field I may never see,
with old trees you make new,
and neighbors that daily
get to see your face.
And though my heart aches
to be divided, I want for you,
as I always have,
your happiest life.
Even if that means you
are only ever here with me
in this heart of mine,
that feels like it could never
beat right for anyone else.
And if it is not my hand
you choose to hold,
I hope she takes care of you,
so that you feel worthy,
the way seed is worthy of soil,
and tides are worthy of the moon.
You are the memory
of a feeling of wholeness,
a love with no skin to shed,
that keeps me company
every hour passed between us.
With you I would want everything.
A long, blessed life, shared
inside seasons that never seem
to drag along, or end too quickly.
But what I have learned about love
most during these years alone,
is that when love is real,
even if it is just on one side,
it exists regardless of anything
that is, or that isn't.

What I Have

may I want what I have
not what I never had

Time

time is a measure
of loss and love

The Abyss

silence can be loud
like the redundant raindrop
that pounds the midnight hour
hard against the surface of night

my feet dig into the bed
holding it how I would you
it is this absence of touch
that spreads my thoughts most

like what do stars do
with the stash of wishes
that for centuries
we have sent them

and how do couples collapse
without making a sound

not all words can be heard
not all moments shared
some endings are not happy

and sometimes the abyss
is the only ground
we have to stand on

Just to Be Seen

Old cigarettes and wine coolers
cluttered the rain pipe,
and on the roof we sat,
strangers pretending to be friends.
She looked at me and said,
"I wish I was you,"
which made me want to scream.
Not even I was me.
I was like the wind, there,
but hollow still,
knocking into leaves
just to be seen.

Pain for Pleasure

for too long now
pain has been
my pleasure

it is our mortal promise
an end for each beginning
beauty blossoms into dust
as we shed before for after
are we merely harbingers
for some future self
that will fly through the wind
of our once aching bones
is it ever our time or always
in the dirt that builds empires
all our faces are the same
and only in the heart then soul
can anything come with us

Truth

your opinion does not
establish my truth

If I Could Fly

where would I go
if I could fly
if fear did not hold
my trembling hand
would I sing
dance moonlight wild
eat a heftier bite
would I love more
or maybe less
would I kiss
a sexy stranger
with a good walk
and a firm grip
or maybe more
would I know
would I go
would I try

Our Memory

we may never
make new memories
but no one can take
away the ones we have

Bridled

I was born with fire in my bones
my body like amber holding fossils
of the stars that once held me
I was meant for more than less
this pallor my skin has settled for
while my desires starve themselves
my passionate heart needs to play
not wither within this celibate crypt
when did loyalty become betrayal
I bridled to some faceless master

Frozen

parts of me
are still frozen
from when your eyes
turned ice cold

we passed each other tonight
on a road winding with gold
I was in the middle of a sentence
you the middle of a life
I know nothing about
my seat was not empty
your eyes still are beautiful
how I wish it were I there
with you in that car
having a conversation
while holding your hand
where do I belong
if not next to you

The Problem

I did not get angry or even
everyone says I should
at the mention of your name
bristle with outrage
that only will I let you go
when how you turned off and away
be how I remember you
the problem is I love you
I have from the start
and my heart unfortunately
does not have an off switch

And Does

I need a man
who says I do
and does

So?

choose the person
who sees your faults
and says "So?"

choose the one
who has been
searching
for you

Don't Forget

we all matter

Do the snails we raised in planters on our porch
by some young oak with Spanish moss remember us,
or the heron in the lake beside the Shakespeare theater,
where in the dusk light grass we played Boggle?

Do the walls of all our homes that hung our pictures
remember the words we shared only with each other,
or the floor the comfortable sound of our laughter
as in turn we cracked coconuts open against the tile?

Are our names still etched in hearts around the world,
like that rainbow monkey hostel elevator in New Zealand,
or that hidden gazebo where we became college sweethearts?

Does that Paris park bench hold in wood our promises,
or the sand on the Cape the impression of our feet,
as hand in hand we walked from the sunrise of one year,
into the sunset of another, until our last?

I look to the wind sometimes, to remind me of our words,
how it felt to talk with someone who knew all my secrets
and chose to love me anyway, but all I see is air.

Are we remembered by anyone but me? If I let you go,
will it be like we never even happened?

Hurting

I wonder if I will
ever stop hurting myself,
in an effort to heal.

Real

I never wanted perfect,
I just wanted real.

Dignity

Dignity is an important human need, that too often is denied. To create intimacy with another person, whether that be emotional or physical, is a sacred act, and when someone leaves our lives, by choice or circumstance, there rarely is the necessary ceremony to support those left behind. I think this is why heartbreak can be so destructive. These days terms like "ghosting" and "blocking" are so common they kind of normalize callous behavior. Of course not every relationship, especially romantic, can be lifelong, but why has it become okay to dismiss, and discard people like objects?

We should not use, or abuse, other people. Life is hard enough. It takes a lot of courage and openness to let someone into your heart, life, body, and story, some of us only do it a few times in our entire lives, and we should treat each other better. Kinder. With more empathy and compassion. How we would want to be treated. Otherwise all we will have left are battered and scarred people, who can no longer trust, and who have no idea what was or is real.

I do not want people in my life who put on the face of perfect, but people who treat themselves and others with the dignity to be honest, even when it is difficult or scary. Who offer closure, and understanding, and are real in the moment. I want to know where I have stood, and where I stand. On a planet that by nature is social, how else can we feel certain, or safe to be ourselves?

Without dignity, how will we ever heal?

In My Dreams

when will I
stop seeing
your face
in my dreams

Stepping Stone Woman

I have only ever been
the stepping stone woman,
the rock someone I love
uses to get to someone else,
but I deserve in this lifetime
the love I have given out,
to at least once be the person
someone has been waiting for,
even if that person is me.

Lucky

These words may seem to you weak,
like without your love I am nothing,
but that is not what I see when I look at me.

At 10,000 feet I dove out of a plane.
As a kid I beat a room full of adults at Scrabble.
I have performed in front of hundreds,
the seven instruments I can play,
and off a mountain I ran to ride five rapids.
I have held a tarantula and an alligator,
been published by the New York Times,
I have won decades of battles with disease.
I swam the Great Barrier Reef in a storm,
I survived enormous trauma
to graduate magna cum laude
and backpack months around the world.
I started my own business at nine,
and saw the Grand Canyon at dawn.
I have built a happy and supportive home,
where alone I raise my beautiful child,
and this is just some of what makes me awesome.

I may miss you and what in love we shared,
but loving you does not make less of me.
I am a strong and passionate woman,
who forgives where others forget,
these words are not my submission
that you were right to leave me.
I write my pain to eradicate it,
and I know anyone who has my love
is lucky.

Whose Heart Beats for Me

My heart beats steady
as a standing clock,
I would have been yours
until the final hour,
but your silence is finally louder
than all the words you spoke,
so it is time to clean house
of what no longer brings joy,
like ill-fitting garments
and years of unreturned love.
I need to make space for the one
whose heart beats for me.

Invisible

I tried to shrink myself
to a size more lovable,
until my giant self
became so small
I was invisible.
How cruel we can be
to the beautiful beasts
that within us live.

I Am Who I Am

I am who I am
love me or hate me
but please stop
trying to change me

Less Brightly

The sun still rose this morning,
but less brightly without you.

The Prayer of a Wishful Heart

I thought your eyes were green,
and then brown,
that maybe you would be tall,
and smart,
with rough edges
and a kind heart,
that beside you I would feel safe,
and within your arms
I would feel home,
that we would make
children with love,
and years with laughter,
growing old together
and not apart,
that you would be different
than I thought,
but everything I needed,
your hand in mine,
until the end of the line.

But now I hope only
that you exist
and not just in memory,
or the prayer
of a wishful heart.

Death

Death
is a cruel
part of life.

Tired

The middle of the night
woke me up again this morning,
like rhinos charging my walls.
The din bored into my sacred space,
stealing whatever stillness
the day leaves me with each night.
I am so soul achingly tired.
Pains blur together,
assaulting my system,
and even 3am holds
nothing more than noise –
words I would rather forget,
wishes that will never come true,
wrongs that cannot be made right.
Feeling like a failure is easy,
during these pillaging moments.
Sometimes thriving is surviving
yet another unforgiving second.

I Don't Know

The older I get,
the less I realize
I know for certain.

The Parts That Do Not Flower

I walk down a road,
fresh with blossoms –
andromeda, lilacs,
lilies-of-the-valley,
buds alive and awake,
reminding me of summer.
So much of who I am
feels like it is sleeping,
waiting for a season
that never comes.
Is that the dream,
or am I, the parts
that do not flower?
What becomes of these
stillborn desires,
all this passion
that never opens its eyes?
Will I ever know?
Can I?

Satisfied

There will always be more.
More beauty, more youth, more fame.
More to choose from, more to have.
So if there is a next time,
I hope to be with someone, who,
with me, and us, is satisfied.

Hard to Believe

It is hard to believe
that all you are now
is a memory.

The Present I Want

I want a present
that is filled
with more future
than it is past.

Undeserving

Sometimes,
the people
we love most,
least deserve
our love.

Do I Have a Sound

The morning came,
dappled with light,
like the wind
in an instrument
about to play.
Can you see my breath?
Do I have a sound?
Am I like the quiet
of this steady room,
or am I the music
that inside my heart
the sun daily makes?

All I Ever Wanted

And all I ever
wanted you to say
was, "It is you.
It will always be you."
And for you to mean it.

Afraid

you are so afraid
nobody will choose you,
but you pull away
before anybody can.

Disparity

how can one person
feel so much
and another person
not feel anything?

Too Soon

you ended the conversation
in the middle of our sentence

The Angel Without Wings

You were a beautiful season that has passed
and I need to somehow distance myself from you,
not from lack of love, but because of how much I care.
I love you as if you had never left,
but I am a prisoner to the fantasy
of what could have been
had you felt the same.
You cannot continue to be
my first thought every morning,
and my last thought every night.
We were meant to meet and make a life,
you were the angel without wings
that gifted me with future,
and every time I look at him
I see all that is good about you,
but you are no longer good for my heart,
and wishing for your return will not make it happen.
I could have loved your burly, stubborn self,
that thunders through this world,
full of holes, and lies, and anger,
until we reached the end of the road,
I could have married you,
you were the easiest decision I ever made,
and if you ever want back into my life,
you are welcome to use the front door,
but I have to believe my story does not end with you,
and that if I can make enough room,
maybe the person who has been waiting for me,
will find me.

So Many Changes

and when there are
so many changes,
that nothing feels familiar,
how are we supposed
to feel at home?

Other Than Yourself

I wonder if you ever
think of me, and us,
but that would mean
you would have to
think about anyone
other than yourself.

Bite Marks

These emotions have teeth,
and all over my heart
are bite marks.

I Reach for You

I bounce between truths,
like a ball that
never hits the ground.
Silent and weightless,
but heavy still
with the gravity of desire.
I reach for you.
Who or what you are,
I no longer know,
only that you are there,
somewhere so close
but also out of view.
And I am here.
Forever falling.
My soul calling your name.

Misfit

all misfits want,
is a place we fit

Holding On

The hope
that the person
we knew
will return
keeps us
holding on

I Choose You

and if I had said
"I choose you"
would it have
made a difference?

Unbroken

I cannot wait
for the day,
when broken
is no longer
the landscape
of my heart.

Rise or Fall

Maybe, for the fact
that we never
had the chance
to rise or fall,
that in a way,
despite how real
you have been
to my waiting heart,
you were mostly
only a fantasy,
I believed you
could have been it.

Hearts Are Not Garbage

I think it is
a sad reflection
of our times,
how normalized
it has become
to throw away people.
Hearts are not garbage
and it takes enormous
courage to care,
when all of us
have suffered.
We do not become
better humans
by ghosting,
cloaking,
and blocking,
we lose connection
this way,
and our global capacity
to trust, and love,
is crippled.
Every living being
is special,
with a rich history,
and landscapes
of emotion.
Not one of us
deserves
to be treated
as anything
less than
sacred.

There is no I.
There is a we.
We are inhabiting this planet,
and how we look at ourselves
in relationship with the world, needs to change.

We are a dynamic and interconnected system of energy and exchange, and every time we allow another child to be slaughtered, we all suffer. I am so tired of acts of violence, hatred, and cruelty, that diminish our collective worth as a species. My son should not have to grow up in a world where toddlers are abducted and brutalized, where it is permissible for six-year-olds to be shot down in school, a world that says it is acceptable for people to be judged by the arbitrary and unimportant color of their skin. This me versus them mentality is primitive and destructive. Nobody is less than. And it needs to stop. I no longer want to see some family or community being torn apart by guns, politics, or prejudice.

All of our cultures, all of our faces,
all of our difference, this is what
makes each individual country,
and our world
as a whole
great.

Did You Know

I wonder if you knew,
when you told me
to write about my pain,
that would include you.

Broken Children

so many adults
are broken children
trying to be whole

A Boat Full of Holes

A relationship
built with lies,
is like a boat
full of holes.

The Echo of Love

Maybe, if I saw you again,
I would not feel the same way.
Maybe, you are like the echo,
of a once spectacular love.

Pieces

I wonder how we get back
the pieces of ourselves
we give to other people?

One-Way Struggle

Love should not be a struggle,
or a one-way declaration of devotion.

Someone New

You make me wonder
what it would be like
to be with someone new.

From Nightmares

Dreams can grow
from nightmares.

Love Should Not

I may not know much about love,
but I know it should not lie,
nor should it make us wait
so long we question our worth.

The End Came

The end came
in the middle
of our story.

Left

You left so completely,
I wonder sometimes if you
were ever even really there.

Down

The problem with
getting our hopes up,
is that the only
place they have to go
from there is down.

Fantasy

at this point,
you are much more fantasy,
than you ever were reality.

The Winds of Sorrow

Churlish
are the winds
of sorrow
that rap
at heart's content.

Doors

It got to the point
where all I was doing
was opening doors,
and all you were doing
was closing them.

Too Often Things End

Too often things end
before they have
had the chance
to really begin.

Questioning

If you find yourself questioning
the way that you matter,
you don't matter
the way that you should.

With

Not everyone
we grow up with,
are we meant
to grow old with.

Losing You

The thought
of losing you again
makes me feel
like I cannot breathe.

I sat quiet in the corner,
a shy sliver of a girl.
My skin was too tight
for my soul
but I preferred to shrink
into invisibility,
than be seen
to be laughed at,
or threatened
for walking the wrong hall.
I swallowed down words,
my questions and feelings,
the things I wanted to try,
and what I wanted to know.
I learned then
how loud silence can be.
Collapsed onto myself,
it was my feet
that walked me forward,
into a life unmuted.
I still hold back,
parts of me stuck
in that spectral space,
but at least now
I have a voice.
At least here,
I make a sound.

Gravity

Like gravity
we sink into
some people
so fully
that without them
we are weightless.

Distance

you keep me
at a distance,
when all I want
is to have you close

Talk of Forever

and for all that time,
and talk of forever,
we didn't even end up
being friends

Where There Is Future

With some people,
all there is, is past.
Choose the ones
where there is future.

Things I Miss (During a Pandemic)

Talking for hours on the phone with a guy I like
Being pregnant
My grandparents
Going for walks on my favorite beach
Southern sweet tea
Dancing with someone
Being kissed, and held, and just all of that
Visiting a new place, or one I love well
Hugs
The crinkle at the corner of someone's eyes, when they talk
A room full of smiles
Cafés in Europe
Seeing a musical
Being touched
Passport stamps
Chinese dumplings
Live music at a restaurant, or concert
Oaks with Spanish moss
Sunflower and poppy fields, in Italy
Skating on trails with my son
Feeling safe, just to be outside
Reasons to celebrate
A really good tiramisu
Milk stout at a craft beer tasting
Searching for treasure, at a book festival
Onion rings from Bahama Breeze
Mini golf
Disney
Being wanted
Getting wet on a water slide
Rotisserie chicken from the side of the road, in Tahiti
My grandmother's pot roast
Singing with my grandfather at the piano
Seagulls over my head on a beach day
Sleeping well at night
Getting my hair cut at a salon
Before my son knew the word "pandemic"

Being someone's go to person
Tree frogs and their mystical song
Picnics in the park
When more of us were healthy

Give It Up

Sometimes,
it has just been
too much
for too little
for too long,
and it is time
to give it up.

A Memory Can't

A memory can't
hold you at night.

Desert Heart

What is there to say
when the words run dry,
the heart a desert
of what it once was?

Silence Says

Silence can say
so many things,
but not all
of them are true.

One of Many Memories

one day, someone will hold you
like they mean it, and love you
in such a way that you forget
there ever was a time without,
and all this pain and loneliness,
that right now feels like everything,
will become one of many memories,
woven into the fabric of your life.

Of My Own Becoming

Sometimes all there is is noise,
and other times only silence.
Somewhere in between I am,
not there or here, or in or out.
Just the phantom of another time
I am not even sure exists really.
Am I the dream, or nightmare
of my own becoming, and do I
honestly care to know.

With Bourbon

Some truths
taste better
with bourbon.

A New Song

The past is a melody
I have played on repeat,
but I need a new song.

Either

It seems, I either shrink down,
so I am not enough for myself,
or I am myself,
and I am too much for others.

Like Fire

Passion burns my veins,
coursing through me like fire,
with no place to go, but within.

In the Center

sometimes, the fog sneaks in
to places that once were light,
and it is hard to clearly see
the difference between
what is left, and what is right.
but in that thick and misty maze,
that can make liars of our eyes,
and blur the lines of our hearts,
we still are there, in the center.

Who Comes Forward

step back
and see
who
comes forward

Not Ready

I am not ready
for the end to come
before so many things
have begun.

Lonely Road

Love should never be
a one-way road.

A Time and Place for Us

the clock strikes infinity,
and I wonder, will there ever be
a time and place for us,
outside of my heart?

Currency

when lies are currency,
the truth isn't worth much

Some Days

Some days, nothing feels good
and nothing feels right,
and everything just feels
too scary, too uncertain,
too much to understand,
and figure out, all by myself.
On these days, I want to hide,
somewhere I will never be found,
and it takes everything I have
to believe I am good enough
to even deserve to exist.

Not You

I have swiped
through thousands
of faces
but every time
"Not you."

The Difference Between Us

the difference
a word makes

one in four billion
one of four billion

the difference
between me and you

Derelict Dream

maybe I am
wrong about you
and everyone else
is right

maybe you are
a derelict dream
and not
my happily ever after

Unsure

I am unsure
whether
it hurts more
that you matter
or that I don't

Carried

I could not walk
the blood in my leg
sick
so for miles
in heat
sticky with flies
you carried me
so I could live.

I wonder if
you carry
any part of me
with you now.

A Whole Life

In the space between us,
we have lived a whole life.

Expectations

Don't expect someone
who isn't honest
with themselves,
to be honest with you.

Apart

Silence
can rip
a heart
apart.

Helpless

We can't help
who our hearts
beat for.

Pretend

Most people don't
want to be loved
for who they are,
they want to be
admired for who
they pretend to be.

Easier

Why is it
so much easier
to know things
than feel them?

Impossible

what is easy for you
might be impossible for me

Sitting Alone

my wish for you
is that love
will never leave you
sitting alone
at the cafeteria table

Love and Breath

being asked
to stop loving you
would be like
being asked
to stop breathing

Will Never Be

everything you are
will never be enough
for someone
who doesn't want you

Wishing I Were Someone Else

I don't want
to be with someone
who goes to sleep each night
wishing I were someone else.

Love Is Not Enough

one of the biggest lessons
that life has taught me
is that love is not enough

Etching Longing

these feelings
cut into my heart
tiny blades
etching longing
for something
that may never
be mine

Only Lies

What if we don't tell the truth,
and we tell only lies,
like I'm moving on,
and I won't always love you

The Worst Pain

I
finally
hear
your
silence.

She

and when I dream,
I am she,
the one who
holds you at night,
and by you is held

Without Words

what is being said
without words?

The Mist of Lost Faces

please don't fade
into the mist
of lost faces

Over Time

every dishonest relationship
degrades and dissolves
over time

It Needs Room

why are you here
in this heart
you did not want
it needs room
without you in it

Out of the Storm

I feel like I am
waiting always
for the wind
to lift me
out of the storm

Apex Predator

who is
the apex predator
within yourself,
making it
impossible
for you
to thrive

Empty Seat

Everywhere I go,
there is an empty seat,
where you should be.

Sweeping Into Trees

we are like wind
sweeping into trees
to be touched

What Makes the Wind

I wonder if the wind feels the absence of touch like I do,
if that is why it swirls and spins,
into clouds and other things.
Does it long for belonging like we? To be seen?
Even if it in essence is always invisible.
Does it wish every moment for the right touch?
And is it aware always of what is missing?
The color, form, and substance,
that it is naturally without.
I wonder if that is why I write here.
To sweep into trees, so to speak.
To even in memory, feel touched,
in the way that gave form to my heart,
thoughts, and feelings.
To be with, in a way that finally felt right,
and not be so substantially without.
Do I record these words,
like a gust of windy emotion,
in case it is only in memory that I
will ever feel that specific way again? I wonder.
If the wind had a heart,
I wonder what it would beat for.
Or if, every time we see it,
fluttering flower petals
and rolling ocean waves,
there but also not there,
it does have a heart,
that though invisible,
still beats for us all,
and whatever it is that we dream about,
during quiet moments, when we are alone.
Does it carry our wishes with it?
Is that what the wind is actually made of?

Unlasting

It is hard
when a dream
comes true but
does not last

Waves

The bad isn't over.
There will be nights
you are lying in a robe on your bed,
screaming silence into a room unfilled,
as the emptiness rips tears
from your aching eyes.
Life never stops hurting.
Pain squats inside the heart,
refusing sometimes ever to fully leave,
especially when time cannot make sense of space.
But this moment right now is a wave.
It will come. And it will go.
And because the good isn't over either,
perhaps what flows in next will be worth you holding on.

The Cord

If the cord
between us
was ever cut,
would I not
then always
be drifting.

Left Wanting

I want you.
I only want you.
And if I am ever
with anyone else,
it will only be because
you didn't want me.

The Night Knows

The night
knows more
of my secrets
than anyone else
ever will.

Built and Broken

Dreams are built,
and hearts are broken,
by things
that are said,
but not meant.

Temporary Interest

Don't confuse
temporary interest
for permanent caring.

Too Painful a Truth

To be
a good
enough reason
for someone
to leave,
but not
a good
enough reason
for someone
to stay,
maybe that
is simply
too painful
a truth
to accept.

Insufficiency

should winter
strip me
of one thing,
let it be
this feeling
of insufficiency

The Sound of Surrender

what does it feel like,
the sound of surrender,
is it a whisper,
or a scream,
to let go so completely
as to allow whatever
is meant to come,
and to go,
to not fight the tides,
or question the stars,
to open our arms,
and ground our fears,
to be steady as a heartbeat,
and free as a breath

Reaching for Rain

I feel my roots
reaching for rain.
It has been
dry for too long.
I am trapped
inside this drought,
with only
the memory
of water.

Reflection of Beauty

I see beauty everywhere.
In petals lush with light.
In the tender fragrance
of dewy morning trees.
In a quiet winter meadow
soft with snowflakes.
And the skeleton of a deer
on a wind stripped beach.
It is the scent of a hug
I know well as my own breath.
And it is clouds covering my
imagination with shapes.
I see beauty in sorrow.
It is inside the pain that
shifts us like tectonic plates.
And the rage that seeks to
protect the battered heart.
But do I belong to this world
full of beautiful things.
Because the mirror only shows
me the shadows of myself,
and my heart lacks the courage
to fill my reflection with love.

Choose Love

Choose love
even when
love doesn't
choose you.

Hope

I don't know why things happen as they do.
I know my experiences, and what my heart feels,
but I have also never been wanted how I want,
or loved that way, and I am not sure I ever will be.
I know how hollowing that thought can be,
in the late night hours, that are full of shadows, and dreams.
But I do believe in love. Still. I feel it.
If we can feel the way we have,
for people who may not even want us in their lives,
imagine what we could offer people who do.
These are the thoughts I hold on to.
That somehow things will work out.
Because when hope dies, so do we, a little.
We lose big chunks of the magic we were born with.
And life starts to lose some of its luster.
And when everything seems so dark
it can be hard to find our way,
think of how the Milky Way
has the same chemical composition as raspberries.
How even the deepest parts of space,
that are absent of color, form, and gravity,
and are so distant they can barely be seen,
still have within them things that are comforting, and familiar.
That is how I see hope.
It is there, almost embedded in the space between us,
allowing us to see when we are blind,
because it doesn't use eyes,
or even any of the other senses.
Hope is a heart driven experience,
a testament of life, and light beyond the darkness.
Don't stop believing that one day
someone will show up in your life,
who will let you know absolutely
that you matter to them in a forever kind of way,
and they are staying. No matter what.
People can surprise us, and they do.
I was surprised this year. In a delightful way.

And that will undoubtedly continue to happen, for you and me.
Our stories aren't over. We are still in them.
And just as likely that things won't work out, they also might.
At least I hope for that. To have a present and future
filled more with gain than loss,
and hopefully to never lose anyone I love again,
except when it is our eventual time to pass on.

I wish your heart an abundance of love.

*Love will not
exclude you.*